Walk in the Sunshine of God

A Letter from Heaven

Written by Stephanie Marchelos

Illustrated by Hannah Hansen

Walk in the Sunshine of God

A Letter from Heaven

Dedicated to my niece
Nikoleta Valentina

My Dear,

When God sees you He sees beauty and His beloved creation.

When you look at the wild flowers be reminded of His amazing creation in which you are one of them.

As the flowers grow without toil so will you: so do not be anxious about anything for the Lord your God will always be with you.

You are so very loved.

Inspired from Matthew 6:28, Philippians 4:6, Isaiah 41:10 NIV

My Dear,

When you wake up in the morning, remember His light will guide you and keep you safe.

The warmth of the sun will comfort you and may it remind you to always walk in the sunshine of God.

When you look to the mountains be reminded that it was His hands who formed them. The same hands that made the earth created your beautiful face .

You are very precious to Him.

Inspired from John 8:12, Amos 4:13, 2 Corinthians 1:3 NIV

My Dear,

When you see a snowflake, remember that there are no two alike. The same is true for every single one of God's children.

He made each child in His image with divine intention and loving care. There are no mistakes in His creation, for everything He made has a purpose.

You are unique; there is no one like you in the universe.

Inspired from Isaiah 64:8 and Genesis 1:27 NIV

My Dear,

When a storm is surrounding you, remember that He is with you wherever you go.

He is always watching over you so that no darkness will harm you.

So whenever you feel afraid, call upon Him, and He will bring you peace.

You are always protected.

Inspired from Isaiah 41:10, John 14:27, Psalm 86:5 NIV

My Dear,

When you hear the birds sing and see the flowers bloom, remember how God has blessed you.

He has given you many different talents, all of which are good and make him very happy.

So let your light shine before others, and use your gifts to glorify Him.

You are gifted.

Inspired from 1 Peter 4:10-11, James 1:17, Psalm 96:1 NIV

My Dear,

When you hear the sound of the ocean waves, remember God's strength. The ocean is just a glimpse of His greatness and sovereignty. Lean on Him; He will renew you and uphold you with his mighty hand.

Never be shy to talk to Him about your worries and weaknesses, for He is gracious. He listens to you and wants a close relationship with you.

He not only listens to your voice He knows your heart.

Inspired from Psalm 145:18-19, Exodus 34: 14, Ephesians 1:11, Jeremiah 29:12-13 NIV

You are
precious,
loved,
gifted,
unique
important,
protected,
& you are His.

My Dear,

   Remember that you hold an extraordinary place in God's heart, and His love for you is endless.

   Even before you were born, God knew and adored you; He knit you together in your mother's womb and called you his own. He knows how many hairs are on the top of your head, your favorite song, and all the desires of your heart.

   He loves you with an everlasting love that no one can ever steal from you.

   Remember that Jesus and his angels are always with you everywhere you go. Call on Him to guide you, and walk in the sunshine of God, always, my dear.

Love,

Nouna

writing inspired from Psalm 91, Psalm 139 Jeremiah 31:3 NIV

*Your journey
has just begun,
my dear one*

"For I know the plans I have for you," declares the LORD," plans to prosper you and not to harm you, plans to give you hope and a future."

Jeremiah 29:11 NIV

I wrote this sweet little book as a reminder to all children and adults how loved we are by Christ our King. I pray this writing of mine shows and reminds you of who you are in Christ.

My inspiration comes from my niece Nikoleta. She has showed me how wonderful and amazing our God is. Our children are our future, every single one has a unique purpose in this world, but I believe it is up to us to show them and guide them in the right direction.

Sincerely,

Stephanie Marchelos

Printed in the United States
by Baker & Taylor Publisher Services